Saturnalia Manifestation Magick

Saturnalia Manifestation Magick

Matthew Petchinsky

Saturnalia Manifestation Magick: A Guide to Unlocking Abundance During the Solstice

By: Matthew Petchinsky

Introduction

Saturnalia, one of the most celebrated festivals of ancient Rome, stands as a testament to the human need for joy, liberation, and renewal during the darkest days of the year. Originally held in honor of Saturn, the god of agriculture, wealth, and time, Saturnalia marked a time of abundant feasting, gift-giving, and the suspension of societal norms. Masters served their slaves, grudges were cast aside, and laughter replaced toil. It was a time to let go of restrictions and invite the light of abundance and renewal into one's life.

The themes of Saturnalia remain just as relevant today as they were centuries ago. In our modern world, we are often caught in cycles of work, stress, and stagnation, struggling to align with our true desires. Saturnalia provides the perfect opportunity to pause, reflect, and shift the narrative. By integrating the festival's energy with modern manifestation practices, we can align with the cosmos, release what no longer serves us, and welcome abundance and transformation into our lives.

This guide is more than just a celebration of an ancient tradition. It is a roadmap for harnessing the energy of Saturnalia to manifest your deepest desires and dreams. Through these pages, you will learn how to honor Saturn's gifts of discipline and transformation while embracing the joy, spontaneity, and abundance of the festival. Saturn, often misunderstood as a stern and unyielding figure, is actually a powerful ally in manifestation. His energy helps us lay strong foundations, focus our intentions, and embrace the gifts of patience and reward.

Saturnalia coincides with the Winter Solstice, the longest night of the year and a pivotal point in the celestial calendar. The Solstice symbolizes both an ending and a beginning—a time to reflect on the darkness within and without, and to celebrate the return of the light. The burning of the manifestation paper on this night creates a profound synergy between your intentions and the cosmic forces at work, turning your desires into tangible results.

In this book, you will discover how to:

- Understand and align with the historical and spiritual significance of Saturnalia.
- Use Saturnalia's unique energy to craft powerful intentions and rituals.
- Connect deeply with Saturn and the transformative power of the Winter Solstice.
- Engage in modern magickal practices, such as creating manifestation papers, burning ceremonies, and spells, to amplify your results.

The manifestation paper included within these pages is not merely a piece of parchment; it is a sacred tool, imbued with your desires and ready to carry your intentions to the universe. Writing on this paper, you will channel your hopes and dreams into a symbolic act of creation, and as it burns, you will release them to the cosmos. The Winter Solstice, with its ancient ties to renewal and light, magnifies this act, ensuring your intentions are heard.

Whether you are a seasoned practitioner of magick or new to the idea of manifestation, this guide will meet you where you are and take you further. It blends ancient rituals with modern techniques, offering a holistic approach to transformation. Each chapter is designed to build upon the last, providing you with the knowledge, tools, and confidence to make this Saturnalia your most transformative yet.

Prepare yourself for a journey that blends history, spirituality, and personal empowerment. As you work through this book, remember that Saturnalia is not just a festival; it is a mindset—a celebration of abundance, release, and renewal. The energy of this season is a gift waiting to be embraced, a chance to set your intentions aflame and watch them take root in the fertile soil of the coming year.

Let Saturnalia guide you toward your truest desires. Let Saturn's wisdom and the Winter Solstice's light pave the way for your transformation. And let this be the year you truly align with the cosmos and manifest the life you have always envisioned. Saturnalia's gifts await you—open your heart, set your intentions, and celebrate the season of abundance and joy.

Chapter 1: Saturnalia Secrets: Unlocking the Power of the Festival

Saturnalia, the ancient Roman festival dedicated to Saturn, the god of agriculture, wealth, and time, was one of the most joyous and anticipated events of the year. Celebrated in mid-December, it marked a period of liberation, abundance, and renewal—a time when social norms were overturned, and the constraints of daily life were replaced with revelry and generosity. To fully unlock the power of Saturnalia for your modern manifestation practices, it is important to understand its origins, traditions, and profound spiritual themes.

The Origins and Traditions of Saturnalia

The roots of Saturnalia trace back to the Roman Republic, where it began as a one-day agricultural festival. Over time, it grew into a week-long celebration that became synonymous with joy and abundance. Held in honor of Saturn, the god who taught humanity the secrets of agriculture and ushered in a mythical golden age of prosperity, the festival symbolized the rebirth of light and life during the darkest days of winter.

Key traditions of Saturnalia included:

- **The Ritual of the Temple of Saturn:** The festival began with a public sacrifice at Saturn's temple in Rome, followed by a banquet open to the public. This act of communal feasting highlighted the themes of shared abundance and gratitude.
- **Role Reversal:** One of the most striking aspects of Saturnalia was the temporary suspension of societal norms. Slaves and masters exchanged roles, symbolizing equality and the breaking of hierarchical boundaries.
- **Gift-Giving:** Exchanging gifts was a core tradition of Saturnalia. Popular gifts included candles (symbolizing light returning after the Solstice), small figurines, and tokens of good luck.
- **Feasting and Merriment:** Families and communities came together to enjoy lavish feasts, drink wine, and play games.

- **Symbolic Decorations:** Homes were adorned with evergreen boughs, wreaths, and garlands, symbols of life and renewal even in the depths of winter.

The joyous and carefree spirit of Saturnalia, coupled with its themes of abundance and renewal, makes it a perfect template for modern manifestation practices.

Themes of Saturnalia: Fuel for Modern Manifestation Practices

The traditions of Saturnalia carry timeless themes that align perfectly with the principles of manifestation:

1. **Abundance:** Saturnalia's feasts, gifts, and celebrations symbolize the universe's infinite abundance. This theme teaches us to shift our mindset from scarcity to plenty, recognizing that there is always enough for everyone.

2. **Reversal and Liberation:** The role reversals during Saturnalia remind us to break free from limiting beliefs, restrictions, and societal pressures that hold us back. Liberation is a key to manifestation—when we free our minds, we open the door to new possibilities.

3. **Joy and Gratitude:** The unbridled joy and generosity of Saturnalia highlight the power of gratitude and positive energy. Manifestation thrives when we express gratitude for what we have and radiate joy toward what we desire.

4. **Renewal and Light:** Saturnalia's alignment with the Winter Solstice underscores the importance of letting go of the old to make room for the new. Burning your manifestation paper on the Solstice mirrors this cycle, releasing old energies and inviting fresh opportunities.

By embracing these themes, you can use Saturnalia as a powerful framework for manifestation, aligning your intentions with the energy of abundance, joy, and transformation.

Preparing Your Space and Mind for Saturnalia Magick

To fully harness the magick of Saturnalia, you must create an environment—both external and internal—that resonates with its energy. Here's how to prepare:

1. **Set the Stage with Decor and Ambiance:**
   - Decorate your space with symbols of Saturnalia, such as evergreen wreaths, candles, and golden accents.
   - Place images or statues of Saturn on your altar to invoke his energy.
   - Use warm, inviting lighting to create a celebratory and sacred atmosphere.

2. **Gather Tools for Rituals and Spells:**
   - Collect candles in festive colors such as gold, green, or red to represent abundance, renewal, and joy.
   - Choose crystals like citrine (for prosperity), amethyst (for clarity), and black tourmaline (for release).
   - Prepare your manifestation paper by infusing it with your energy—write your name or sigil on it to personalize it.

3. **Cleanse Your Space:**
   - Use smoke cleansing with herbs such as rosemary, sage, or frankincense to clear stagnant energy.
   - Play uplifting music or use sound bowls to fill your space with positive vibrations.

4. **Prepare Your Mind and Spirit:**
   - Meditate to center yourself and connect with Saturnalia's energy. Imagine yourself surrounded by abundance, joy, and light.

- Reflect on the themes of release and renewal. Write down what you want to let go of and what you want to call into your life.

5. **Set Your Intentions:**
    - Write your desires on the manifestation paper included in this book. Be specific and visualize these intentions as already fulfilled.
    - Place the paper on your altar or sacred space, ready to be burned on the Winter Solstice.

6. **Engage in Saturnalia Festivities:**
    - Invite joy and gratitude into your life by celebrating with loved ones. Cook a festive meal, exchange small gifts, and play games to honor the spirit of the festival.

Saturnalia's secrets lie not only in its rich history but also in its ability to inspire joy, liberation, and abundance. By understanding its origins, embracing its themes, and preparing your space and mind, you can unlock the festival's transformative power for your own manifestation journey. Saturnalia is more than a celebration—it is a gateway to aligning with the universe's limitless potential

Chapter 2: The Manifestation Blueprint: Crafting Your Saturnalia Intentions

Manifestation is the art of turning thoughts into reality by aligning your energy, emotions, and actions with your desires. During Saturnalia, this practice becomes even more potent because the festival's themes of abundance, joy, and liberation naturally amplify manifestation efforts. By crafting your intentions with clarity and purpose, you harness the transformative energy of Saturnalia and the Winter Solstice to bring your dreams into existence.

This chapter will guide you through the principles of manifestation, provide a step-by-step process for identifying and writing your desires, and show you how to align your intentions with Saturnalia's themes of prosperity and release.

The Principles of Manifestation

Manifestation is not simply about wishing for something and waiting for it to appear. It's a deliberate process that involves focus, energy, and alignment. Understanding these core principles will set the foundation for your Saturnalia manifestation practice:

1. **Clarity is Key:** The universe responds to specificity. Vague desires yield vague results. Be clear and concise about what you want.
   - Instead of saying, "I want more money," try, "I want to earn $10,000 by March 1st through my creative projects."
2. **Focus on the Feeling:** Manifestation works best when you not only visualize your desire but also feel the emotions associated with achieving it. Imagine the joy, relief, or excitement you'll experience when your goal becomes reality.
3. **Release Limiting Beliefs:** Doubts and fears act as energetic blockages. Saturnalia's themes of liberation can help you identify and release these barriers.
4. **Take Inspired Action:** Manifestation isn't passive. While intention is powerful, action grounds your desires in the physical world. Use Saturnalia to set the stage for actionable steps.
5. **Trust the Process:** Patience and faith are vital. Trust that the universe is working in your favor, even if you don't see immediate results.

By understanding these principles, you'll be ready to take the next step: crafting your Saturnalia intentions with precision and power.

Step-by-Step Guidance: Identifying and Writing Your Desires

Crafting your Saturnalia intentions is a sacred process. Treat it as a ritual in itself, infusing your words with focus, energy, and purpose. Follow these steps to create a manifestation paper that resonates deeply with your goals:

Step 1: Reflect on Your Desires

- **Identify What You Truly Want:** Take time to reflect on what you genuinely want to manifest. This could be related to wealth, relationships, health, personal growth, or spiritual fulfillment.
- **Be Honest with Yourself:** Your intentions should align with your true desires, not what others expect of you. Ask yourself, "What would truly make me happy and fulfilled?"
- **Focus on Abundance, Not Lack:** Frame your desires in terms of what you want to attract, not what you want to avoid. For example, instead of saying, "I don't want debt," say, "I am financially free and thriving."

Step 2: Write with Clarity and Power

- **Be Specific:** Detail your desires clearly. Include specifics such as amounts, dates, or qualities. The more vivid your intention, the easier it is for the universe to deliver.
- **Use Present Tense:** Write as though your desire has already been achieved. For example, "I am enjoying my dream job that allows me to travel the world."
- **Incorporate Emotion:** Add words that convey the joy or gratitude you'll feel when your manifestation comes to life. For example, "I am deeply grateful for my thriving business that brings me financial freedom."

- **Keep It Concise:** While details are important, avoid overcomplicating your intentions. A clear, focused statement is most effective.

Step 3: Visualize as You Write

- As you write your manifestation paper, close your eyes and visualize your intention. Imagine every detail—what you see, hear, and feel when your desire becomes reality.
- Envision the energy of Saturnalia, abundant and joyful, infusing your words with power.

Step 4: Empower Your Words with Magickal Energy

- **Draw Symbols or Sigils:** Add symbols of Saturn, such as a sickle or a star, to your paper for extra energy. You can also create a personal sigil that represents your intention.
- **Anoint Your Paper:** Use oils associated with abundance (such as patchouli or cinnamon) to anoint the corners of your paper.
- **Charge with Crystals:** Place crystals like citrine or pyrite on your manifestation paper to amplify its energy.

Aligning Your Intentions with Saturnalia's Themes

Saturnalia's unique energy enhances manifestation by focusing on abundance, joy, and release. Align your intentions with these themes for maximum impact:

1. **Abundance and Prosperity:**
   - Saturnalia's feasting and gift-giving remind us that the universe is infinitely abundant. Let your intentions reflect this mindset.
   - Example Intention: "I am enjoying an abundant life filled with wealth, love, and opportunities."

2. **Reversal and Liberation:**
   - Use Saturnalia's theme of role reversal to let go of old beliefs and step into a new version of yourself.
   - Example Intention: "I release all doubts and step into my power as a confident and successful person."

3. **Joy and Gratitude:**
   - Saturnalia's festivities highlight the importance of gratitude. Expressing gratitude in advance for your manifestation reinforces its energy.
   - Example Intention: "I am deeply grateful for the vibrant health and joy I experience every day."

4. **Release and Renewal:**
   - The Winter Solstice and Saturnalia symbolize the end of one cycle and the beginning of another. Include an intention to release what no longer serves you.
   - Example Intention: "I release all fear and welcome new opportunities with open arms."

Tips for Crafting the Perfect Manifestation Paper

- **Write by Hand:** Handwriting your intentions imbues them with your energy and makes the process more personal.
- **Use Quality Paper:** Choose parchment or another high-quality material to honor the sacredness of the process.
- **Keep It Focused:** If you have multiple desires, write each on a separate piece of paper to keep the energy clear.
- **Store with Intention:** Keep your manifestation paper in a sacred space, such as an altar or a special box, until the Winter Solstice.

Crafting your Saturnalia intentions is a powerful act of creation. By combining the principles of manifestation with the themes of Saturnalia, you align yourself with the universe's energy of abundance and renewal.

Chapter 3: Rituals of Light: Honoring Saturn and the Solstice

Saturnalia and the Winter Solstice present a powerful convergence of energies—abundance, transformation, and the return of light. By honoring Saturn, the god of agriculture, time, and renewal, and aligning your rituals with the celestial rhythms of the Solstice, you can amplify your intentions and create a profound spiritual experience. This chapter guides you through a step-by-step ritual, the use of candles, crystals, and herbs, and how to synchronize your practices with the Winter Solstice for maximum manifestation power.

A Guided Ritual to Connect with Saturn's Transformative Energy

Saturn's energy is both grounding and transformative, helping you lay the foundation for long-term success while releasing what no longer serves you. This ritual is designed to honor Saturn, invite his blessings, and channel his energy into your manifestation work.

Step 1: Prepare Your Sacred Space

1. **Cleanse the Space:** Begin by cleansing your ritual area to remove stagnant or negative energy. Use smoke cleansing with sage, cedar, or frankincense, or sprinkle salt water around the perimeter of your space.
2. **Set Up an Altar:** Create a simple altar dedicated to Saturn. Include:
   - A statue or image of Saturn (or a representation, such as a sickle or hourglass).
   - Candles in black (symbolizing release), gold (abundance), and white (purity and renewal).
   - Crystals such as obsidian, onyx, and citrine.
   - Offerings like wine, bread, or coins to honor Saturn.

3. **Create a Circle of Protection:** Stand in your space and visualize a glowing circle of light surrounding you. This circle will keep you grounded and protected during the ritual.

Step 2: Invoke Saturn's Energy

1. Light the black candle and say:
   "Great Saturn, Keeper of Time and Giver of Abundance, I call upon your presence. Teach me to release the past, embrace discipline, and sow the seeds of my desires."
2. Meditate for a moment, visualizing Saturn's energy—a steady, grounding force wrapping around you. Imagine his golden sickle cutting away negativity and clearing space for growth.
3. Place your hands on your altar or over your heart and state your intention for the ritual. Speak with clarity and conviction. For example:
   "I honor Saturn and align with his wisdom to manifest abundance, joy, and transformation in my life."

Step 3: Engage in the Saturnalia Manifestation Ritual

1. Write your manifestation intention on the special paper prepared earlier. Focus on one clear and specific goal.
2. Place the paper under a gold candle and say:
   "With Saturn's guidance, I plant this seed of intention in the fertile soil of the cosmos. May it grow strong and true."
3. Light the gold candle and meditate on your intention. Visualize it as already fulfilled. Feel the joy and gratitude of achieving your desire.
4. Light the white candle and say:
   "As the Solstice brings the return of light, so too does my intention bring renewal and abundance into my life."

Step 4: Conclude the Ritual

1. Close the ritual by thanking Saturn:
   "Great Saturn, I thank you for your wisdom, guidance, and blessings. May your energy continue to guide my path."
2. Extinguish the candles in reverse order: white, gold, then black, symbolizing completion and grounding.
3. Keep the manifestation paper on your altar or in a sacred space until the Winter Solstice burning ceremony.

Using Candles, Crystals, and Herbs for Manifestation
Candles:
Candles are powerful tools for focus and intention. In this ritual:

- **Black candles** represent release and transformation. Use them to banish negativity and clear the way for new growth.
- **Gold candles** symbolize abundance, success, and the blessings of Saturn. Use them to amplify your desires.
- **White candles** signify renewal and the return of light. Use them to purify your energy and bring clarity.

Crystals:
Crystals amplify energy and provide specific vibrations for your ritual:

- **Obsidian and Onyx:** Grounding stones that help release negative energy and protect your intentions.
- **Citrine:** A crystal of abundance, manifestation, and joy.
- **Clear Quartz:** An all-purpose amplifier that enhances the energy of other tools.

Place these crystals on your altar, hold them during meditation, or use them to charge your manifestation paper.

Herbs:

Herbs carry symbolic and energetic properties that enhance your ritual:

- **Frankincense:** Promotes spiritual connection and purification.
- **Rosemary:** Protects and clears the mind for focused intention.
- **Bay Leaves:** Write wishes on bay leaves and burn them to release your intentions to the universe.
- **Cinnamon:** Adds energy, success, and speed to your manifestations.

Burn these herbs as incense, add them to your offerings, or use them to dress your candles.

Aligning Your Ritual with the Winter Solstice

The Winter Solstice, the longest night of the year, represents both an ending and a beginning. It is a powerful time to release the old and welcome the light of new opportunities. Aligning your Saturnalia ritual with the Solstice enhances its potency.

Key Steps for Solstice Alignment:

1. **Timing:** Perform the ritual on the Solstice night or within the three days surrounding it, when the energy of renewal is strongest.
2. **Burning Ceremony:** On the Solstice, burn your manifestation paper as a symbolic release of your intention. This act sends your desires into the cosmos and signifies your trust in the process.
3. **Meditation:** After burning the paper, meditate on the return of the light. Visualize your intentions taking root and growing with the lengthening days.
4. **Celebrate:** End the ritual with a joyful act, such as feasting, singing, or sharing gratitude with loved ones. This mirrors Saturnalia's themes of abundance and joy.

Honoring Saturn and the Winter Solstice through rituals of light connects you to ancient wisdom and cosmic rhythms. By combining candles, crystals, and herbs with intentional practices, you create a powerful manifestation process that aligns with the transformative energy of Saturnalia. The ritual not only sets your intentions into motion but also fosters a deeper connection to the universal cycles of release and renewal. Let this ceremony guide you toward your desires and illuminate your path in the coming year.

Chapter 4: The Manifestation Paper: Writing Your Future

The manifestation paper is one of the most powerful tools in your Saturnalia ritual. It serves as a physical representation of your intentions, acting as a bridge between your inner desires and the external reality you wish to create. By writing your goals, dreams, and aspirations on this paper, you infuse them with your energy and focus. The act of burning it during the Winter Solstice transforms your intentions into a sacred offering, releasing them into the universe for fulfillment.

This chapter explores the significance of the manifestation paper, provides a step-by-step guide to charging it with your energy, and explains how to prepare it for the Solstice burning ceremony.

The Significance of Writing on the Manifestation Paper

Writing is a transformative act. It translates your thoughts and emotions into something tangible, giving form to your abstract desires. Here's why the manifestation paper is so significant:

1. **Clarity and Focus:** Writing your intentions forces you to clarify what you want, helping you focus your energy on specific goals. This sharpens your manifestation process, making it more effective.

2. **Symbolic Power:** The paper becomes a symbolic container for your desires. It holds the energy you pour into it, acting as a talisman for your manifestation ritual.

3. **Energetic Amplification:** By writing with intention and emotion, you infuse the paper with your personal energy, creating a strong connection between you and your desires.

4. **Release and Trust:** Burning the paper during the Solstice symbolizes release. It shows your trust in the universe to bring your desires to fruition, freeing you from attachment to the outcome.

Ritual Steps for Infusing the Paper with Your Energy

Infusing the manifestation paper with your energy is an essential part of the ritual. This process ensures that your intentions are charged with your personal power and aligned with the universe.

Step 1: Create a Sacred Writing Space

1. **Cleanse Your Space:** Use sage, palo santo, or incense to cleanse the area where you'll write your intentions. This removes negative energy and prepares the space for your work.
2. **Gather Your Tools:** Have your manifestation paper, a pen (preferably one with gold or black ink), and any ritual tools like candles, crystals, or herbs nearby.
3. **Set the Mood:** Light candles and play soft, meditative music to create a peaceful and focused environment.

Step 2: Center Yourself

1. **Meditate:** Sit quietly for a few minutes and focus on your breath. Visualize a golden light surrounding you, connecting you to Saturn's energy and the abundant energy of Saturnalia.
2. **Focus on Gratitude:** Reflect on what you're grateful for. Gratitude raises your vibration and aligns you with the energy of abundance.

Step 3: Write Your Intention

1. **Start with Clarity:** Begin by writing your name or a personal symbol (such as your astrological sign or a sigil) at the top of the paper. This links the paper to your unique energy.
2. **Write in the Present Tense:** Phrase your intention as if it has already come to pass. For example:
   ◦ Instead of "I want a new job," write, "I am thriving in my dream job that brings me joy and financial abundance."
3. **Be Specific:** Include as much detail as possible. For instance, if you're manifesting a financial goal, specify the amount and the timeframe.
4. **Invoke Emotion:** Describe how achieving this intention makes you feel. Include words like joy, gratitude, or peace to anchor your desires in positive emotions.
5. **Keep It Concise:** Focus on one or two main intentions to avoid diluting your energy.

Step 4: Charge the Paper

1. **Hold the Paper:** Place your hands over the paper and close your eyes. Visualize your intention as a glowing orb of light within your heart.
2. **Infuse the Paper:** Imagine this light traveling down your arms and into the paper. See the words you've written glowing with energy and power.
3. **Speak Your Intention:** Read your intention aloud with confidence and conviction. This vocal affirmation adds another layer of energy to the paper.

Step 5: Enhance with Ritual Tools

1. **Candles:** Pass the paper over the flame of a gold or white candle to purify and charge it. Be mindful not to let it catch fire.
2. **Crystals:** Place crystals like citrine, clear quartz, or amethyst on the paper to amplify its energy.
3. **Herbs:** Sprinkle a small amount of herbs associated with your intention (such as cinnamon for success or rosemary for clarity) onto the paper.

Preparing the Paper for the Solstice Burning

The act of burning the manifestation paper on the Winter Solstice is deeply symbolic. It transforms your written intentions into smoke and ash, sending them to the universe for fulfillment. Preparing the paper for this ceremony ensures that it's ready to serve its purpose.

Step 1: Fold the Paper with Intention

1. Fold the paper neatly, visualizing your intention being sealed within it.
2. If desired, fold it into a specific shape, such as a triangle (symbolizing manifestation) or a square (symbolizing stability).

Step 2: Store the Paper in a Sacred Space

1. Place the folded paper on your altar or in a special box. Surround it with symbols of Saturnalia, such as candles, evergreen sprigs, or gold coins.
2. Keep it safe until the Solstice, allowing its energy to build.

Step 3: Prepare for the Burning Ceremony

1. **Choose Your Space:** Decide where you'll perform the burning ceremony. An outdoor space under the night sky is ideal, but a safe indoor area with a fireproof container works as well.
2. **Gather Tools:** Have a lighter or matches, a cauldron or fireproof bowl, and additional items like incense or candles ready for the ceremony.

Step 4: Set Your Intentions for Release

As you prepare for the burning ceremony, reflect on the themes of the Winter Solstice—release, renewal, and the return of light. Visualize the smoke from your paper carrying your desires into the universe.

The manifestation paper is more than a ritual tool; it is a sacred vessel for your dreams and intentions. By writing your future with clarity, charging the paper with your energy, and preparing it for the symbolic act of burning, you create a powerful connection to the transformative energy of Saturnalia and the Winter Solstice. This simple yet profound practice bridges the gap between intention and reality, turning your desires into tangible results.

Chapter 5: Burning Away the Old, Embracing the New

The Winter Solstice burning ceremony is the culmination of your Saturnalia manifestation ritual. It is a sacred act of release and renewal, symbolizing the end of one cycle and the beginning of another. By burning your manifestation paper, you send your intentions into the universe, trusting in its infinite wisdom to manifest your desires. This chapter provides a detailed guide to performing the ceremony, explores the symbolic use of ashes as a reminder of transformation, and outlines steps to remain open and aligned with your goals after the ritual.

The Winter Solstice Burning Ceremony: A Guide to Releasing Your Intentions

The Winter Solstice, the longest night of the year, is a time of profound transformation. It marks the moment when darkness begins to recede and light returns, mirroring the themes of release and renewal central to your ritual.

Step 1: Prepare for the Ceremony

1. **Choose the Right Time and Place:**
   - The ceremony is best performed on the night of the Solstice or within three days of it.
   - Select a quiet, safe location, ideally outdoors under the night sky or in a well-ventilated indoor space with a fireproof container.

2. **Gather Your Tools:**
   - Your manifestation paper.
   - A lighter or matches.
   - A fireproof bowl, cauldron, or a small outdoor fire pit.
   - Candles (white for renewal, gold for abundance, black for release).
   - Optional: Incense or herbs like rosemary, sage, or bay leaves to enhance the energy.

3. **Set the Mood:**
   - Create an ambiance with soft music or silence. Light candles or hang string lights to symbolize the return of light.
   - Cleanse the space with smoke cleansing or salt to ensure it is free of negative energy.

Step 2: Create a Sacred Circle

1. Stand in your chosen space and visualize a glowing circle of light forming around you. This circle represents protection and focus.
2. If you wish, call upon Saturn or other spiritual allies to join you in the ritual:
   "Great Saturn, Keeper of Time and Giver of Abundance, I invite your presence. Bless this ceremony as I release the old and welcome the new."

Step 3: Set Your Intentions for Release

1. Hold your manifestation paper in your hands and close your eyes. Visualize your intentions glowing on the paper, vibrant and alive with energy.
2. Speak your intentions aloud, affirming your trust in the process:
   "I release these desires into the universe, trusting in its infinite power to manifest them in perfect timing."
3. Reflect on what you are letting go of—fears, doubts, or old habits—and declare their release:
   "I release all that no longer serves me. I welcome transformation and renewal."

Step 4: Burn the Manifestation Paper

1. Light the black candle (symbolizing release) and use it to ignite the paper. Place the burning paper in your fireproof container.
2. As the paper burns, watch the flames consume your words. Visualize your intentions transforming into smoke and rising to the universe.
3. Say:
   "As this paper turns to ash, my intentions are carried to the cosmos. I release them with trust and gratitude."

Step 5: Meditate and Give Thanks

1. After the paper has fully burned, sit in silence or meditate for a few moments. Feel the light of renewal filling you as you embrace the energy of the Solstice.
2. Thank Saturn or the universe for its guidance and blessings:
   "Thank you, Saturn, for your wisdom. Thank you, universe, for receiving my intentions and guiding me toward their fulfillment."

How to Use the Ashes as a Symbolic Reminder of Transformation

The ashes left behind from the burning ceremony are powerful symbols of release and transformation. Here are some ways to use them:

1. **Scatter Them Outdoors:**
   - Return the ashes to the earth by scattering them in your garden, under a tree, or in flowing water. This act symbolizes surrendering your intentions to the natural cycles of the universe.

2. **Incorporate Them Into a Ritual:**
   - Mix the ashes with soil and use it to plant a seed or sapling. As the plant grows, it represents the manifestation of your desires.

3. **Create a Protective Talisman:**
   - Place the ashes in a small pouch or vial and keep it on your altar or carry it with you. This serves as a reminder of the transformation you initiated.

4. **Anoint Your Tools:**
   - Mix the ashes with oil or wax to create a sacred anointing balm for candles, crystals, or other ritual tools.

What to Do After the Ceremony to Remain Open to Receiving Your Desires

Manifestation doesn't end with the burning ceremony—it requires continued openness and alignment. Here are steps to stay connected to your intentions:

Step 1: Trust the Process

- Release attachment to the outcome. Trust that the universe is working behind the scenes to align your desires with the right opportunities and timing.
- Avoid overthinking or second-guessing your intentions.

Step 2: Take Inspired Action

- While the universe supports you, your efforts matter. Look for opportunities, make decisions, and take steps that align with your goals.
- For example, if you manifested financial abundance, create a budget, apply for a new job, or launch a project.

Step 3: Stay Grateful

- Gratitude keeps your energy aligned with abundance. Each day, reflect on the blessings you already have and the progress you're making.
- Consider keeping a gratitude journal to document your manifestations as they unfold.

Step 4: Maintain Your Energy

- Practice self-care and grounding activities, such as meditation, yoga, or time in nature, to keep your energy balanced and receptive.

- Surround yourself with positive influences, including people, environments, and media that inspire you.

Step 5: Celebrate Small Wins

- Acknowledge and celebrate the small signs of progress. The universe often delivers manifestations in stages, so honor each step as it comes.

The burning ceremony is a transformative act of release, trust, and renewal. By burning away the old and embracing the new, you align with the powerful energies of Saturnalia and the Winter Solstice. Let the ashes remind you of the change you've initiated, and continue to walk your path with faith, action, and gratitude. Your desires are already in motion—trust in their arrival.

Appendix A: Saturnalia Symbols and Their Modern Meanings

Saturnalia is rich with symbols that hold deep cultural, spiritual, and magickal significance. These symbols, rooted in ancient traditions, can be used to enhance your rituals and deepen your connection to the festival's transformative energy. Each symbol embodies a specific aspect of Saturnalia, such as abundance, renewal, or liberation. This appendix explores these symbols, their modern meanings, and practical suggestions for incorporating them into your magickal practices.

1. Saturn's Sickle

Historical Significance:

The sickle is a symbol of Saturn's agricultural domain, representing his role as the god of harvest and time. In Roman mythology, Saturn taught humanity the secrets of agriculture, using the sickle to reap the bounty of the earth.

Modern Meaning:

- **Harvest and Abundance:** The sickle represents the rewards of hard work and the harvesting of intentions planted earlier in the year.
- **Cutting Away the Old:** It symbolizes the removal of negativity, outdated beliefs, and obstacles that hinder growth.
- **Cycles of Time:** The sickle reminds us of life's cyclical nature and the importance of aligning with cosmic rhythms.

Incorporating into Rituals:

- Place a sickle or a small symbolic representation on your altar to honor Saturn's transformative energy.
- Visualize the sickle cutting away negativity during meditation or energy-clearing rituals.
- Use a ceremonial knife (athame) as a modern stand-in for the sickle in your rituals.

2. Evergreen Wreaths
Historical Significance:

Evergreens, used to decorate homes during Saturnalia, symbolized life and renewal in the midst of winter. Their enduring green color represented resilience and hope for the return of spring.

Modern Meaning:

- **Renewal and Resilience:** Evergreen wreaths remind us of our inner strength and the promise of renewal.
- **Eternal Life:** They symbolize the continuity of life and the cyclical nature of the seasons.
- **Unity:** The circular shape of a wreath represents wholeness and harmony.

Incorporating into Rituals:

- Hang an evergreen wreath in your ritual space to invite the energy of renewal and resilience.
- Adorn wreaths with gold ribbons or small charms to amplify prosperity and abundance.
- Use a wreath as a focal point for meditative visualization, imagining your life in perfect harmony and balance.

3. Gold Coins
Historical Significance:

Gift-giving was central to Saturnalia, and gold coins (real or symbolic) were often exchanged as tokens of prosperity and good fortune.

Modern Meaning:

- **Abundance and Wealth:** Gold coins represent financial prosperity and the flow of abundance into your life.
- **Gratitude:** They symbolize the value of generosity and the rewards of giving.

- **Manifestation Energy:** Their reflective surface amplifies intentions related to success and achievement.

Incorporating into Rituals:

- Place gold coins on your altar to draw financial abundance and success.
- Use a gold coin as a talisman by carrying it in your wallet or placing it in a manifestation jar.
- Include coins in offerings to Saturn during your Saturnalia rituals, asking for his blessings of wealth and prosperity.

4. Candles

Historical Significance:

Candles were commonly exchanged as gifts during Saturnalia, symbolizing light and the return of the sun after the Winter Solstice.

Modern Meaning:

- **Illumination:** Candles represent clarity, wisdom, and the light of new beginnings.
- **Transformation:** Fire is a symbol of purification and the transformative power of intention.
- **Energy and Vitality:** The flame of a candle embodies life's energy and the spark of creation.

Incorporating into Rituals:

- Light gold candles to attract abundance, black candles to banish negativity, and white candles to invite renewal.
- Use candles as focal points for meditative visualization, imagining your desires manifesting as the flame grows.
- Anoint candles with oils (such as cinnamon or patchouli) to enhance their magickal properties.

5. Saturnalia Dice (Gaming and Fun)
Historical Significance:

Games of chance were popular during Saturnalia, representing the temporary suspension of societal rules and the playful spirit of the festival.

Modern Meaning:

- **Risk and Reward:** Dice symbolize taking calculated risks and trusting in the flow of life.
- **Luck and Opportunity:** They remind us to stay open to unexpected opportunities and serendipitous moments.
- **Joy and Playfulness:** Dice encourage embracing joy, fun, and spontaneity.

Incorporating into Rituals:

- Use dice in divination to seek guidance on decisions or opportunities.
- Roll dice as part of a ritual to symbolize taking a chance on your dreams.
- Include dice as altar decorations to invite playful energy into your manifestations.

6. Laurel Leaves
Historical Significance:

Laurel leaves were symbols of victory and accomplishment in Roman culture, often worn as wreaths by victors and leaders.

Modern Meaning:

- **Success and Triumph:** Laurel leaves signify the achievement of goals and the celebration of personal victories.
- **Protection:** They are associated with shielding against negativity and ensuring success.

- **Recognition:** Laurel leaves remind us to honor our accomplishments and the progress we've made.

Incorporating into Rituals:

- Burn dried laurel leaves to release intentions or seek clarity during meditation.
- Add laurel leaves to your altar as a symbol of success and victory.
- Write your desires on a bay leaf (a type of laurel) and burn it to release your intention to the universe.

7. Saturnalia Feast Foods (Bread, Wine, Fruits)

Historical Significance:

Feasting was a central part of Saturnalia, symbolizing abundance and communal celebration. Bread, wine, and fruits were staples of the feast, honoring Saturn's agricultural blessings.

Modern Meaning:

- **Gratitude:** Feast foods symbolize appreciation for the earth's bounty and the fruits of your labor.
- **Community:** They represent connection, unity, and shared abundance.
- **Harvest Energy:** Foods used in rituals connect you to the cycle of planting, growing, and reaping.

Incorporating into Rituals:

- Offer bread, wine, or fruit to Saturn on your altar as part of your Saturnalia ritual.
- Share a feast with loved ones to embody the spirit of generosity and joy.
- Use fruits like pomegranates or apples in rituals to symbolize fertility and renewal.

8. Evergreen Trees
Historical Significance:

Evergreen trees, decorated with symbols and offerings, were central to Saturnalia celebrations, embodying life and resilience.

Modern Meaning:

- **Eternal Life:** Evergreen trees remind us of nature's enduring strength and vitality.
- **Renewal and Fertility:** They symbolize growth and the return of life after winter's dormancy.
- **Connection to Nature:** Evergreen trees encourage grounding and alignment with the natural world.

Incorporating into Rituals:

- Decorate an evergreen tree with symbols of your intentions, such as ribbons, coins, or ornaments.
- Meditate near an evergreen tree to connect with its grounding and renewing energy.
- Use small sprigs of evergreen as altar decorations or as part of spellwork for resilience and growth.

Conclusion

The symbols of Saturnalia carry deep magickal significance and provide a tangible way to connect with the festival's transformative energy. By incorporating these symbols into your rituals, you amplify your intentions and align with the ancient wisdom of Saturnalia. Let these symbols guide and inspire you as you embrace abundance, joy, and renewal in your magickal practice.

Appendix B: Saturnalia Spell Recipes

Saturnalia is a time of abundance, joy, and renewal, and its energy can be harnessed to craft powerful spells that align with the themes of the season. The following recipes are designed to enhance your connection to Saturnalia's transformative energy, amplify your manifestations, and protect your space as you move into the new year. Each spell incorporates symbols and traditions of Saturnalia to bring prosperity, happiness, and protection into your life.

1. Spell for Abundance: The Golden Coin Prosperity Spell

Purpose: To attract financial prosperity and abundance into your life.

Ingredients:

- A gold coin (real or symbolic, such as a gold-painted coin or charm)
- Green and gold candles
- Cinnamon powder or essential oil
- A small pouch or jar
- A bay leaf

Instructions:

1. **Prepare Your Space:** Cleanse your ritual area with sage or incense. Place the green and gold candles on your altar or workspace.
2. **Charge the Coin:** Hold the gold coin in your hands and visualize it glowing with a golden light. Speak your intention:

"This coin is a magnet for prosperity. It draws abundance and wealth into my life."

3. **Anoint the Coin:** Dab a small amount of cinnamon oil or sprinkle cinnamon powder on the coin, saying:
   "With the warmth of cinnamon, my fortune grows. Abundance flows freely to me."

4. **Write on the Bay Leaf:** Write a specific financial goal on the bay leaf (e.g., "$10,000 by March"). Place the bay leaf and the coin into the pouch or jar.

5. **Seal with Candle Wax:** Light the green and gold candles. Drip a few drops of wax onto the pouch or jar to seal your intention.

6. **Place in a Sacred Space:** Keep the pouch or jar on your altar or in a safe place where you'll see it regularly. Visualize its energy working for you whenever you pass by.

2. Spell for Joy: The Evergreen Gratitude Charm
Purpose: To infuse your life with joy, positivity, and gratitude.
Ingredients:

- A small sprig of evergreen (pine, fir, or cedar)
- A yellow candle
- A piece of yellow or gold ribbon
- Lavender essential oil or dried lavender flowers
- A piece of parchment paper and pen

Instructions:

1. **Prepare Your Evergreen Sprig:** Hold the evergreen sprig and anoint it with lavender oil or sprinkle dried lavender over it.
2. **Write Your Gratitudes:** On the parchment paper, write three things you are grateful for and three things that bring you joy.
3. **Wrap the Sprig:** Roll the parchment paper around the evergreen sprig and tie it securely with the ribbon, saying:
   "Evergreen of life, lavender of peace, joy and gratitude, may they never cease."
4. **Charge with Candlelight:** Light the yellow candle and pass the charm through the flame's glow (be careful not to burn it), visualizing a golden light of joy filling your life.
5. **Carry or Hang:** Carry the charm with you or hang it in your home to invite positivity and gratitude into your space.

3. Spell for Protection: Saturn's Shield of Light

Purpose: To create a protective barrier around yourself or your home, invoking Saturn's energy for stability and security.

Ingredients:

- A black candle
- A small mirror
- Rosemary and sage (dried or fresh)
- A bowl of salt
- A piece of black string or cord

Instructions:

1. **Cleanse the Space:** Burn rosemary and sage to cleanse your ritual area. Place the mirror in the center of your workspace.
2. **Create a Salt Circle:** Sprinkle salt around the mirror, forming a protective circle.
3. **Invoke Saturn's Protection:** Light the black candle and say:
   "Great Saturn, shield me from harm. Let your wisdom and strength be my charm. Protect my space, my mind, my heart. Let your energy guard every part."
4. **Bind the Intention:** Tie the black string around the mirror, creating a binding of protection. As you tie the knots, visualize a shield of light surrounding you or your home.
5. **Place the Mirror:** Place the mirror near your front door or in a prominent location to reflect negativity away from your space.

4. Saturnalia Oil for Manifestation

Purpose: To anoint candles, tools, or yourself to enhance manifestation energy.

Ingredients:

- Carrier oil (such as olive, almond, or jojoba oil)
- Cinnamon sticks
- Orange peel
- Frankincense resin or essential oil
- Gold glitter (optional for festive energy)
- A small glass bottle or jar

Instructions:

1. **Infuse the Oil:** Place the cinnamon sticks, orange peel, and a few drops of frankincense oil into the bottle. Fill the bottle with the carrier oil.
2. **Bless the Oil:** Hold the bottle in your hands and say:
   "Oil of light, oil of power, charge this blend to manifest and empower. Abundance flows, intentions rise, as Saturn's wisdom fills the skies."
3. **Use in Rituals:** Use the oil to anoint candles, your manifestation paper, or even your wrists and temples during Saturnalia rituals.

5. Seasonal Offering for Saturn

Purpose: To honor Saturn and seek his blessings for abundance, protection, and wisdom.

Ingredients:

- A loaf of bread (homemade or purchased)
- A small bowl of wine
- Coins (real or symbolic)
- Sprigs of evergreen or laurel

Instructions:

1. **Prepare the Offering Space:** Set up an area on your altar or outside in nature where you'll present the offering. Place the bread, bowl of wine, coins, and evergreens together.
2. **Bless the Offering:** Light a candle and say:
   "Great Saturn, Lord of Time, Keeper of Harvest and Wealth Divine, I offer these gifts in gratitude and trust. Bless my life, my work, my path, and all that I entrust."
3. **Leave the Offering:** Leave the offering overnight on your altar or bury it in nature as a sign of gratitude and alignment with Saturnalia's energy.

Conclusion

These Saturnalia spell recipes harness the season's unique energy, helping you manifest abundance, cultivate joy, and protect your space. By crafting oils, talismans, and seasonal offerings, you deepen your connection to the ancient wisdom of Saturnalia and infuse your magick with the transformative power of this sacred time. Incorporate these spells into your practice to honor Saturnalia's themes and create lasting change in your life.

<u>Message from the Author:</u>

I hope you enjoyed this book, I love astrology and knew there was not a book such as this out on the shelf. I love metaphysical items as well. Please check out my other books:

-Life of Government Benefits

-My life of Hell

-My life with Hydrocephalus

-Red Sky

-World Domination:Woman's rule

-World Domination:Woman's Rule 2: The War

-Life and Banishment of Apophis: book 1

-The Kidney Friendly Diet

-The Ultimate Hemp Cookbook

-Creating a Dispensary(legally)

-Cleanliness throughout life: the importance of showering from childhood to adulthood.

-Strong Roots: The Risks of Overcoddling children

-Hemp Horoscopes: Cosmic Insights and Earthly Healing

- Celestial Hemp Navigating the Zodiac: Through the Green Cosmos

-Astrological Hemp: Aligning The Stars with Earth's Ancient Herb

-The Astrological Guide to Hemp: Stars, Signs, and Sacred Leaves

-Green Growth: Innovative Marketing Strategies for your Hemp Products and Dispensary

-Cosmic Cannabis

-Astrological Munchies

-Henry The Hemp

-Zodiacal Roots: The Astrological Soul Of Hemp

- **Green Constellations: Intersection of Hemp and Zodiac**

-Hemp in The Houses: An astrological Adventure Through The Cannabis Galaxy

-Galactic Ganja Guide

Heavenly Hemp

Zodiac Leaves

Doctor Who Astrology

Cannastrology

Stellar Satvias and Cosmic Indicas

Celestial Cannabis: A Zodiac Journey

AstroHerbology: The Sky and The Soil: Volume 1

AstroHerbology:Celestial Cannabis:Volume 2

Cosmic Cannabis Cultivation

The Starry Guide to Herbal Harmony: Volume 1

The Starry Guide to Herbal Harmony: Cannabis Universe: Volume 2

Yugioh Astrology: Astrological Guide to Deck, Duels and more

Nightmare Mansion: Echoes of The Abyss

Nightmare Mansion 2: Legacy of Shadows

Nightmare Mansion 3: Shadows of the Forgotten

Nightmare Mansion 4: Echoes of the Damned

The Life and Banishment of Apophis: Book 2

Nightmare Mansion: Halls of Despair

Healing with Herb: Cannabis and Hydrocephalus

Planetary Pot: Aligning with Astrological Herbs: Volume 1

Fast Track to Freedom: 30 Days to Financial Independence Using AI, Assets, and Agile Hustles

Cosmic Hemp Pathways

How to Become Financially Free in 30 Days: 10,000 Paths to Prosperity

Zodiacal Herbage: Astrological Insights: Volume 1

Nightmare Mansion: Whispers in the Walls

The Daleks Invade Atlantis

Henry the hemp and Hydrocephalus

10X The Kidney Friendly Diet
Cannabis Universe: Adult coloring book
Hemp Astrology: The Healing Power of the Stars
Zodiacal Herbage: Astrological Insights: Cannabis Universe: Volume 2
<u>**Planetary Pot: Aligning with Astrological Herbs: Cannabis Universes: Volume 2**</u>
Doctor Who Meets the Replicators and SG-1: The Ultimate Battle for Survival
Nightmare Mansion: Curse of the Blood Moon
<u>**The Celestial Stoner: A Guide to the Zodiac**</u>
Cosmic Pleasures: Sex Toy Astrology for Every Sign
Hydrocephalus Astrology: Navigating the Stars and Healing Waters
Lapis and the Mischievous Chocolate Bar

Celestial Positions: Sexual Astrology for Every Sign
Apophis's Shadow Work Journal: : A Journey of Self-Discovery and Healing
Kinky Cosmos: Sexual Kink Astrology for Every Sign
Digital Cosmos: The Astrological Digimon Compendium
Stellar Seeds: The Cosmic Guide to Growing with Astrology
Apophis's Daily Gratitude Journal

Cat Astrology: Feline Mysteries of the Cosmos
The Cosmic Kama Sutra: An Astrological Guide to Sexual Positions
Unleash Your Potential: A Guided Journal Powered by AI Insights
Whispers of the Enchanted Grove

Cosmic Pleasures: An Astrological Guide to Sexual Kinks
369, 12 Manifestation Journal

Whisper of the nocturne journal(blank journal for writing or drawing)

The Boogey Book

Locked In Reflection: A Chastity Journey Through Locktober

Generating Wealth Quickly:

How to Generate $100,000 in 24 Hours

Star Magic: Harness the Power of the Universe

The Flatulence Chronicles: A Fart Journal for Self-Discovery

The Doctor and The Death Moth

Seize the Day: A Personal Seizure Tracking Journal

The Ultimate Boogeyman Safari: A Journey into the Boogie World and Beyond

Whispers of Samhain: 1,000 Spells of Love, Luck, and Lunar Magic: Samhain Spell Book

Apophis's guides:

Witch's Spellbook Crafting Guide for Halloween

<u>Frost & Flame: The Enchanted Yule Grimoire of 1000 Winter Spells</u>

<u>The Ultimate Boogey Goo Guide & Spooky Activities for Halloween Fun</u>

Harmony of the Scales: A Libra's Spellcraft for Balance and Beauty

The Enchanted Advent: 36 Days of Christmas Wonders

Nightmare Mansion: The Labyrinth of Screams

Harvest of Enchantment: 1,000 Spells of Gratitude, Love, and Fortune for Thanksgiving

The Boogey Chronicles: A Journal of Nightly Encounters and Shadowy Secrets

The 12 Days of Financial Freedom: A Step-by-Step Christmas Countdown to Transform Your Finances

Sigil of the Eternal Spiral Blank Journal

A Christmas Feast: Timeless Recipes for Every Meal

Holiday Stress-Free Solutions: A Survival Guide to Thriving During the Festive Season

Yu-Gi-Oh! Holiday Gifting Mastery: The Ultimate Guide for Fans and Newcomers Alike

Holiday Harmony: A Hydrocephalus Survival Guide for the Festive Season

Celestial Craft: The Witch's Almanac for 2025 – A Cosmic Guide to Manifestations, Moons, and Mystical Events

Doctor Who: The Toymaker's Winter Wonderland

Tulsa King Unveiled: A Thrilling Guide to Stallone's Mafia Masterpiece

Pendulum Craft: A Complete Guide to Crafting and Using Personalized Divination Tools

Nightmare Mansion: Santa's Eternal Eve

Starlight Noel: A Cosmic Journey through Christmas Mysteries

The Dark Architect: Unlocking the Blueprint of Existence

Surviving the Embrace: The Ultimate Guide to Encounters with The Hugging Molly

The Enchanted Codex: Secrets of the Craft for Witches, Wiccans, and Pagans

Harvest of Gratitude: A Complete Thanksgiving Guide

Yuletide Essentials: A Complete Guide to an Authentic and Magical Christmas

Celestial Smokes: A Cosmic Guide to Cigars and Astrology

Living in Balance: A Comprehensive Survival Guide to Thriving with Diabetes Insipidus

Cosmic Symbiosis: The Venom Zodiac Chronicles

The Cursed Paw of Ambition

Cosmic Symbiosis: The Astrological Venom Journal

Celestial Wonders Unfold: A Stargazer's Guide to the Cosmos (2024-2029)

The Ultimate Black Friday Prepper's Guide: Mastering Shopping Strategies and Savings

Cosmic Sales: The Astrological Guide to Black Friday Shopping

Legends of the Corn Mother and Other Harvest Myths

Whispers of the Harvest: The Corn Mother's Journal

The Evergreen Spellbook

The Doctor Meets the Boogeyman

The White Witch of Rose Hall's SpellBook

The Gingerbread Golem's Shadow: A Study in Sweet Darkness

The Gingerbread Golem Codex: An Academic Exploration of Sweet Myths

The Gingerbread Golem Grimoire: Sweet Magicks and Spells for the Festive Witch

The Curse of the Gingerbread Golem

10-minute Christmas Crafts for kids

<u>Christmas Crisis Solutions: The Ultimate Last-Minute Survival Guide</u>

Gingerbread Golem Recipes: Holiday Treats with a Magical Twist

The Infinite Key: Unlocking Mystical Secrets of the Ages

Enchanted Yule: A Wiccan and Pagan Guide to a Magical and Memorable Season

Dinosaurs of Power: Unlocking Ancient Magick

Astro-Dinos: The Cosmic Guide to Prehistoric Wisdom

Gallifrey's Yule Logs: A Festive Doctor Who Cookbook

The Dino Grimoire: Secrets of Prehistoric Magick

The Gift They Never Knew They Needed

The Gingerbread Golem's Culinary Alchemy: Enchanting Recipes for a Sweetly Dark Feast

A Time Lord Christmas: Holiday Adventures with the Doctor

Krampusproofing Your Home: Defensive Strategies for Yule

Silent Frights: A Collection of Christmas Creepypastas to Chill Your Bones

Santa Raptor's Jolly Carnage: A Dino-Claus Christmas Tale

Prehistoric Palettes: A Dino Wicca Coloring Journey

The Christmas Wishkeeper Chronicles

The Starlight Sleigh: A Holiday Journey

Elf Secrets: The True Magic of the North Pole

Candy Cane Conjurations

Cooking with Kids: Recipes Under 20 Minutes

Doctor Who: The TARDIS Confiscation

The Anxiety First Aid Kit: Quick Tools to Calm Your Mind

Frosty Whispers: A Winter's Tale

The Infinite Key: Unlocking the Secrets to Prosperity, Resilience, and Purpose

The Grasping Void: Why You'll Regret This Purchase

Astrology for Busy Bees: Star Signs Simplified

The Instant Focus Formula: Cut Through the Noise

The Secret Language of Colors: Unlocking the Emotional Codes

Sacred Fossil Chronicles: Blank Journal

The Christmas Cottage Miracle

Feeding Frenzy: Graboid-Inspired Recipes

Manifest in Minutes: The Quick Law of Attraction Guide

The Symbiote Chronicles: Doctor Who's Venomous Journey

Think Tiny, Grow Big: The Minimalist Mindset

The Energy Key: Unlocking Limitless Motivation

New Year, New Magic: Manifesting Your Best Year Yet

Unstoppable You: Mastering Confidence in Minutes

Infinite Energy: The Secret to Never Feeling Drained

Lightning Focus: Mastering the Art of Productivity in a Distracted World

If you want solar for your home go here: https://www.harborso-lar.live/apophisenterprises/

Get Some Tarot cards: https://www.makeplayingcards.com/sell/apophis-occult-shop

Get   some   shirts: https://www.bonfire.com/store/apophis-shirt-emporium/

<u>Instagrams:</u>
@apophis_enterprises,
@apophisbookemporium,
@apophisscardshop
Twitter: @apophisenterpr1
 Tiktok:@apophisenterprise
Youtube: @sg1fan23477, @FiresideRetreatKingdom
Hive: @sg1fan23477
CheeLee: @SG1fan23477

Podcast: Apophis Chat Zone: https://open.spotify.com/show/ 5zXbrCLEV2xzCp8ybrfHsk?si=fb4d4fdbdce44dec

Newsletter: https://apophiss-newsletter-27c897.beehiiv.com/

If you want to support me or see posts of other projects that I have come over to: **buymeacoffee.com/mpetchinskg**

I post there daily several times a day

Get your Dinowicca or Christmas themed digital products, especially Santa Raptor songs and other musics. Here:
https://sg1fan23477.gumroad.com

Apophis Yuletide Digital has not only digital Christmas items, but it will have all things with Dinowicca as well as other Digital products.